Wearable Tech:
Fashion Meets Functionality

By

Russell H. Merchant

TABLE OF CONTENTS

Introduction

The modern world has witnessed an unprecedented surge in the adoption of wearable technology, marking a significant paradigm shift in how we interact with and integrate technology into our daily lives. From the once simplistic wristwatches that could merely tell time, we have now entered an era where wearable devices have become an extension of ourselves, seamlessly blending fashion and functionality. This book, "Wearable Tech: Fashion Meets Functionality," delves into the captivating journey of wearable technology, exploring the intriguing marriage between cutting-edge innovation and style.

A. The Rise of Wearable Technology:

The rise of wearable technology can be traced back to humble beginnings, where early inventors and visionaries dared to imagine a world where technology could be effortlessly worn rather than merely wielded. As advancements in miniaturization, sensor technology, and wireless communication unfolded, wearable devices began to transcend mere utility and became fashion statements in their own right.

The launch of iconic wearables like fitness trackers and smartwatches introduced the masses to the possibilities of seamlessly incorporating technology into their lifestyles. Health-conscious individuals found solace in the ability to monitor their fitness goals, while others reveled in the convenience of receiving notifications and staying connected on-the-go, all while sporting sleek and stylish wearables.

Moreover, the fashion industry took note of this burgeoning trend, leading to a transformative collaboration between technology companies and renowned fashion designers. The emergence of wearable tech runways and exhibitions further validated the notion that these gadgets could be both functional and fashionable, adding a whole new dimension to personal style.

As we journey through this book, we will explore the evolutionary path of wearable technology, dissecting the driving forces behind its meteoric rise and the impact it has had on society at large. Beyond the fascination of the latest gadgets, we will also uncover the underlying principles of user experience, data privacy concerns, and the potential ethical dilemmas that arise from the fusion of fashion and functionality.

In the following chapters, we will examine the intricate design processes, the convergence of technology and art, and the transformative role of artificial intelligence in shaping the future of wearable tech. Additionally, we will delve into specific applications, such as health and fitness wearables, interactive clothing, and their enthralling implications in entertainment and gaming.

Through "Wearable Tech: Fashion Meets Functionality," we invite you to embark on a captivating expedition into the world of wearable technology. Whether you are a tech enthusiast, a fashion aficionado, or simply curious about the evolution of modern gadgets, this book endeavors to enlighten, inspire, and ignite a passion for the boundless possibilities that lie ahead in the realm where fashion and functionality beautifully coalesce.

B. Intersection of Fashion and Functionality:

Traditionally, the fields of fashion and technology have followed separate trajectories, with fashion emphasizing aesthetics, self-expression, and identity, while technology focused on solving problems and enhancing efficiency. However, the convergence of these domains has led to an extraordinary metamorphosis, giving birth to wearables that not only serve practical purposes but also embody artistry and personal flair.

At the heart of this intersection lies a delicate balance between aesthetics and utility. Wearable technology no longer relies solely on bulky, utilitarian designs; it has evolved into a harmonious blend of form and function. Innovators have come to realize that for wearable devices to be embraced by the masses, they must complement individual style and seamlessly integrate into various aspects of everyday life.

Fashion designers have embraced this new canvas for creativity, finding inspiration in the possibilities offered by technology. The collaboration between technology companies and fashion houses has given rise to wearables that make bold fashion statements while maintaining a high level of functionality. These devices not only perform complex tasks but also elevate the wearer's appearance, becoming coveted accessories in their own right.

This intersection has also transcended the world of fashion, finding applications in diverse industries. From healthcare to entertainment, wearable tech has proven its adaptability, creating novel experiences and enhancing human interactions. It has redefined how we perceive and interact with technology, as it becomes an intimate and integral part of our lives, rather than something we merely interact with through screens.

Throughout this book, we will delve deeper into the innovative minds behind the designs, the engineering marvels that power these gadgets, and the psychology behind their widespread adoption. We will explore how fashion-forward wearables have challenged conventions, inspiring individuals to embrace technology as an expression of their identity and lifestyle.

By examining case studies and real-world examples, we will witness the transformative impact of wearable technology on industries, social norms, and personal well-being. From self-tracking health wearables to interactive clothing that reacts to environmental stimuli, the possibilities are as limitless as the human imagination.

As we embark on this journey through the nexus of fashion and functionality, we invite you to discover the enchanting world of "Wearable Tech: Fashion Meets Functionality." Whether you are a technophile, a fashion enthusiast, or simply curious about the future of technology, this book promises to be a revelation, unearthing the captivating potential of wearables and their profound impact on our lives.

C. Purpose and Scope of the Book:

The purpose of this book is to explore the multifaceted world of wearable technology and its harmonious integration with fashion, unraveling the various layers that make this amalgamation possible. We seek to provide readers with a comprehensive understanding of how wearable tech has evolved from a mere trend into a transformative movement that has redefined the way we interact with technology on a personal level.

Through meticulous research and insightful analysis, we delve into the historical roots of wearable technology, tracing its origins and evolution to the present day. The book unearths the initial attempts and inventions that laid the groundwork for the astonishing array of wearables available today, ranging from smartwatches and fitness trackers to sophisticated interactive clothing.

A central focus of the book is the captivating interplay between fashion and functionality within wearable tech. We examine the collaborative efforts of fashion designers and technology innovators, exploring the creative processes that result in wearables that not only serve practical purposes but also appeal to individual tastes and sensibilities. The chapters dedicated to design and aesthetics will uncover the principles that shape the visual appeal of these devices, making them desirable fashion accessories.

Moreover, the book scrutinizes the vital aspect of functionality and user experience in wearable tech. We explore the core features and functionalities of these gadgets, the technology behind their seamless operation, and the human-centered design principles that ensure a positive user experience. Additionally, we delve into the challenges posed by data privacy and security concerns in the era of wearable tech, examining the ethical considerations that arise from the collection and utilization of personal data.

The scope of this book extends beyond exploring the present state of wearable technology. We peer into the future, delving into potential advancements and applications that have the power to shape the technological landscape. From AI-driven wearables that learn and adapt to users' needs to the integration of wearable tech in diverse industries, we endeavor to paint a vivid picture of the limitless possibilities ahead.

Ultimately, "Wearable Tech: Fashion Meets Functionality" strives to enlighten readers about the exciting confluence of fashion and technology, inspiring a deeper appreciation for the role of wearables in our lives. Whether you are a tech enthusiast, a fashion aficionado, or simply curious about the latest trends, this book offers a captivating voyage into a world where fashion and functionality intertwine to shape the future of technology.

Chapter 1
The Evolution of Wearable Tech

A. Historical Background of Wearable Technology:

The roots of wearable technology can be traced back to centuries ago, where ingenious inventors and thinkers laid the groundwork for the remarkable devices we have today. The concept of wearable tech has its origins in rudimentary tools and accessories that early humans fashioned to serve specific purposes. From the primitive wrist-worn sundials used by the ancient Egyptians to track time to the abacus rings employed by the Chinese for basic calculations, early examples of wearables demonstrate the innate human desire for convenience and efficiency.

Fast forward to the Renaissance period, and we find the emergence of ornamental and functional wearable devices, such as mechanical timepieces worn as pocket watches or pendants. These timekeeping instruments were not only tools of practicality but also symbols of status and craftsmanship. The fusion of fashion and functionality began to take shape as these timepieces became more intricately designed and embellished.

The 20th century saw significant milestones in wearable technology, particularly with the advent of radio communication and the miniaturization of electronic components. In the early 1900s, the invention of the wristwatch by Swiss watchmaker Patek Philippe marked a significant shift in wearable timekeeping. The wristwatch quickly gained popularity due to its convenience and accessibility, gradually becoming a fashion statement rather than just a utilitarian item.

In the latter half of the 20th century, wearable tech took a giant leap forward with the development of calculators, digital watches, and early fitness tracking devices. These gadgets laid the groundwork for the wearable revolution we experience today. In the 1970s, the release of the Hamilton Pulsar, one of the first digital watches, captured the world's imagination and set the stage for the digital wearables that would follow in the coming decades.

The late 20th century witnessed a surge in wearable tech innovations, with the introduction of products like wearable heart rate monitors and personal digital assistants (PDAs). While these early wearables were primarily targeted at specific niches, they sowed the seeds for a technology boom that would transform the way we interact with devices.

The 21st century brought a radical shift in wearable technology. The convergence of smartphone technology, wireless communication, and sophisticated sensors led to the development of smartwatches, fitness trackers, and other wearable devices that seamlessly integrate into our lives. As the devices became more compact, powerful, and aesthetically pleasing, the boundary between fashion and technology blurred, giving rise to a new era where wearables became not only functional but also fashionable.

The historical journey of wearable technology is a testament to human ingenuity and the desire to bring technology closer to our bodies and daily experiences. From humble origins to a multi-billion-dollar industry, wearable tech continues to evolve, offering us glimpses of a future where technology and fashion walk hand in hand, enriching our lives in unimaginable ways.

B. Early Attempts and Inventions:

The concept of wearable technology is not a recent phenomenon but can be traced back to early attempts and inventions that laid the groundwork for the technological marvels we have today. In ancient civilizations, ingenious inventors crafted rudimentary wearable tools and accessories to address specific needs and tasks.

One of the earliest known wearable devices was the abacus ring, which emerged in China around 300 BCE. The abacus ring was a miniature abacus that could be worn on a finger, allowing individuals to perform basic calculations conveniently. This early example of wearable tech demonstrated the human inclination towards making technology portable and easily accessible.

As we move through history, we find other remarkable attempts at wearable technology. In the 16th century, the Nuremberg egg was crafted by Peter Henlein, considered one of the world's first watchmakers. The Nuremberg egg was a small, egg-shaped watch that could be worn as a pendant or attached to clothing. This innovative timekeeping device marked a significant advancement in portable timekeeping and laid the foundation for future wrist-worn timepieces.

The 19th century witnessed the rise of pocket watches, which became popular among the elite during the Victorian era. These intricately designed timepieces were carried in small pockets attached to waistcoats or jackets. Pocket watches blended functionality with elegance, showcasing the potential for fashion-forward wearable accessories.

In the early 20th century, radio communication spurred advancements in wearable technology. In 1907, the "vest pocket" wireless receiver, developed by Nathan Stubblefield, allowed users to wear a wireless device on their bodies and communicate wirelessly. Although these devices were large and cumbersome by today's standards, they represented a significant leap in the evolution of wearables and the idea of being connected while on the move.

As the world progressed into the mid-20th century, the introduction of digital technology paved the way for more sophisticated wearable inventions. The first digital watch, the Hamilton Pulsar, made its debut in 1972. With its futuristic LED display, the Pulsar captured the public's imagination and marked the transition from traditional analog timepieces to digital wearables.

Another notable early attempt at wearable technology was the heart rate monitor. In the 1970s, Dr. Seppo Säynäjäkangas developed a wireless heart rate monitor that athletes could wear during training. This invention revolutionized fitness tracking and laid the groundwork for modern-day fitness wearables that monitor various health metrics.

These early attempts and inventions paved the way for the wearable revolution that was to come. The combination of technological advancements and creative thinking propelled wearables from simple tools to fashion-forward, multi-functional gadgets that have become an integral part of modern life. As we explore the history of wearable tech, we gain a deeper appreciation for the innovative minds of the past and their contributions to shaping the world of wearable technology we know today.

B. Early Attempts and Inventions:

The journey of wearable technology can be traced back to ingenious early attempts and inventions that set the stage for the technological marvels we enjoy today. From ancient civilizations to the modern era, human creativity has driven the desire to make technology more accessible and integrated into our daily lives.

In ancient times, rudimentary wearable devices were born out of necessity. The ancient Egyptians used wrist-worn sundials to keep track of time during the day, while the Greeks developed the astrolabe, a handheld device that allowed navigation based on the position of celestial bodies. These early attempts at wearables exemplified the human fascination with portable tools that enhanced daily activities.

Fast-forward to the Renaissance period, and we witness the emergence of ornamental wearables that also served functional purposes. Renaissance watchmakers crafted pendant watches, known as "chatelaines," which women wore as accessories around their waist. These exquisite timepieces demonstrated the potential for wearable tech to transcend mere functionality and become symbols of status and beauty.

The 19th century witnessed significant advancements in wearable timekeeping with the advent of pocket watches. These compact and elegantly designed watches could be conveniently carried in small pockets attached to clothing. Pocket watches became a symbol of sophistication and were favored by the elite, further blurring the lines between fashion and functionality.

The turn of the 20th century brought revolutionary inventions, such as the wristwatch, which forever changed the landscape of wearable tech. In 1904, the Brazilian aviator Alberto Santos-Dumont collaborated with Louis Cartier to create a wrist-worn watch that allowed him to track time during flights. This pioneering wristwatch design gained popularity among aviators and civilians alike, eventually leading to the widespread adoption of wristwatches as fashion accessories.

Advancements in wireless communication and electronics in the mid-20th century paved the way for more complex wearable inventions. During World War II, military personnel used "wrist radios" for covert communication in special operations. Although large and cumbersome, these early wrist radios foreshadowed the potential for wearable communication devices in the future.

The 1970s brought about a digital revolution in wearable tech with the introduction of digital watches. The Hamilton Pulsar, released in 1972, was one of the first digital watches available to the public. With its LED display and futuristic design, the Pulsar captured the imagination of consumers and signaled a new era in timekeeping.

These early attempts and inventions, driven by human curiosity and innovation, laid the foundation for the remarkable evolution of wearable technology. From basic tools of convenience to fashion-forward gadgets that seamlessly integrate into our lives, wearables have come a long way. As we explore the historical roots of wearable tech, we gain a deeper appreciation for the inventors and visionaries who dared to imagine a world where technology could be effortlessly worn and stylishly embraced.

C. Technological Advancements Leading to Modern Wearables:

The evolution of wearable technology has been shaped by remarkable technological advancements that have propelled these devices from mere novelties to indispensable companions in our daily lives. As technology steadily advanced, the convergence of miniaturization, wireless communication, and sophisticated sensors paved the way for the modern wearables we know today.

One of the key technological breakthroughs was the development of microelectronics, which allowed for the miniaturization of electronic components. This miniaturization enabled the creation of smaller and lighter devices, making it possible to embed complex functionalities into wearable gadgets without sacrificing comfort or aesthetics.

The advent of wireless communication revolutionized wearable technology. Bluetooth technology, in particular, played a pivotal role in connecting wearables to smartphones and other devices, facilitating seamless data transfer and real-time interactions. The ability to wirelessly sync data and receive notifications on wearable devices transformed them into extensions of our smartphones, enhancing convenience and accessibility.

Advancements in sensor technology played a critical role in the rise of health and fitness wearables. The integration of advanced biometric sensors, such as heart rate monitors, accelerometers, and GPS, enabled wearables to track various health metrics and provide real-time feedback to users. These sensors not only opened new possibilities for fitness enthusiasts but also transformed wearables into valuable tools for monitoring health and well-being.

The proliferation of smart fabrics and flexible electronics further expanded the potential of wearable technology. Smart fabrics, embedded with conductive threads and sensors, allowed for the creation of interactive clothing that could detect and respond to various stimuli, such as changes in temperature or touch. These advancements merged fashion with functionality, giving rise to a new wave of wearable tech that extended beyond traditional devices.

The rise of data analytics and artificial intelligence (AI) has also been instrumental in shaping modern wearables. AI-powered wearables can learn from user behavior, adapt to individual preferences, and offer personalized insights and recommendations. This integration of AI not only enhances user experience but also opens up new possibilities for wearables to become proactive health and lifestyle coaches.

Furthermore, improvements in battery technology have extended the operational lifespan of wearables. More efficient batteries, coupled with energy-saving optimization, ensure that wearables can last longer between charges, enhancing their practicality and user-friendliness.

The convergence of these technological advancements has led to a proliferation of diverse wearables, ranging from smartwatches and fitness trackers to augmented reality glasses and smart clothing. These modern wearables have transcended utility, becoming fashion-forward accessories that seamlessly integrate into our lives.

As we delve deeper into the evolution of wearable tech, we bear witness to the profound impact of these technological innovations, shaping a future where wearable technology continues to revolutionize how we interact with the world around us. The journey from early attempts to modern marvels highlights the relentless pursuit of technological excellence and the boundless possibilities that lie ahead in the dynamic realm of wearable technology.

Chapter 2
Fashionable Tech: Design and Aesthetics

A. The Importance of Aesthetics in Wearable Tech:

In the realm of wearable technology, aesthetics have emerged as a powerful driving force that goes beyond mere superficial appeal. The integration of aesthetics in wearable tech is not merely about making devices visually appealing; it is a crucial aspect that influences user adoption, emotional connection, and the overall success of wearable gadgets.

One of the primary reasons aesthetics are vital in wearable tech is the intimate nature of these devices. Unlike traditional gadgets, wearables are worn on the body, often in close proximity to the user's skin and personal space. As a result, wearables become an extension of one's identity, style, and self-expression. Aesthetics play a pivotal role in ensuring that wearables seamlessly integrate into the user's personal fashion choices and daily life.

Fashion-forward wearables that are visually appealing and align with the user's individual style are more likely to be embraced as desirable accessories rather than merely functional gadgets. Companies that prioritize aesthetics understand that wearables are not solely utilitarian tools; they are fashion statements and expressions of the wearer's personality.

The emotional connection between users and their wearables is also influenced by aesthetics. A beautifully designed wearable elicits positive emotions and attachment, enhancing the overall user experience. Wearables that evoke joy, pride, or a sense of admiration become cherished companions, reinforcing their significance in the user's life.

Moreover, aesthetics play a significant role in breaking down barriers to adoption. Historically, wearable tech faced challenges in achieving widespread acceptance due to bulky, unattractive designs that did not align with mainstream fashion preferences. However, as aesthetics improved and wearables became sleeker, slimmer, and more visually appealing, they gained wider acceptance among diverse user groups.

Design and aesthetics also play a role in addressing the issue of social acceptance. Wearables that closely resemble conventional accessories, such as stylish bracelets or elegant timepieces, are less likely to draw attention and scrutiny from others. This aspect is particularly important in professional settings or social situations where conspicuous tech gadgets may be frowned upon.

Aesthetics extend beyond the physical appearance of wearables; they also encompass the user interface and interaction design. An intuitive and visually pleasing user interface enhances the usability of wearables, ensuring that users can easily navigate through features and functionalities.

In conclusion, aesthetics are a fundamental aspect of wearable technology that goes beyond superficial appearances. The visual appeal of wearables influences user adoption, emotional attachment, and social acceptance. As wearable tech continues to evolve, companies that strike the right balance between fashion-forward designs and seamless functionality are likely to lead the way in shaping a future where aesthetics and technology harmoniously coexist.

B. Integration of Fashion Designers and Technologists:

The seamless integration of fashion designers and technologists has been a transformative force in shaping the world of wearable technology. As wearables evolved from mere gadgets to fashion-forward accessories, collaboration between these two seemingly disparate fields became paramount to strike the perfect balance between aesthetics and functionality.

Fashion designers bring a unique perspective to wearable tech. Their expertise lies in understanding human anatomy, form, and the art of visual storytelling through clothing and accessories. By incorporating fashion designers into the wearable tech development process, wearables transcend their utilitarian roots and become wearable art, reflecting individual style and identity.

Technologists, on the other hand, possess the technical prowess to turn creative ideas into reality. They have a deep understanding of cutting-edge technologies, materials, and engineering principles that form the foundation of wearable devices. Technologists work hand in hand with fashion designers to ensure that wearables not only look appealing but also deliver on performance and usability.

The integration of fashion designers and technologists results in a collaborative synergy that redefines wearable technology. Fashion designers provide valuable insights into current trends, user preferences, and aesthetics that resonate with different demographics. Armed with this knowledge, technologists can develop wearables that cater to diverse tastes while ensuring the devices are functional, reliable, and user-friendly.

This collaboration extends to the very core of wearable tech design. From choosing the right materials to crafting innovative form factors, fashion designers and technologists work together to create wearables that seamlessly blend into users' lives. The emphasis on form and comfort ensures that wearables are not only visually appealing but also ergonomically designed for all-day wear.

Moreover, integrating fashion designers and technologists fosters cross-disciplinary thinking. The fusion of fashion and technology sparks new ideas and innovative concepts that would not have been possible through separate approaches. This cross-pollination of ideas leads to the birth of unconventional wearables that push the boundaries of both fashion and technology.

The success of wearable tech owes much to this collaborative approach. Prominent fashion designers have teamed up with technology giants to launch exclusive lines of smartwatches, fitness trackers, and smart accessories. These fashion-forward wearables have resonated with consumers, driving widespread adoption and acceptance of wearable tech in mainstream markets.

As wearable technology continues to evolve, the integration of fashion designers and technologists will remain a critical aspect. Their collective expertise will shape wearables that not only perform complex tasks but also reflect the ever-changing landscape of fashion and individual expression. By merging creativity and innovation, fashion and technology unite to redefine the possibilities of wearable tech, inspiring a future where style and substance harmoniously coexist.

C. Case Studies of Successful Fashion-Forward Wearables:

Throughout the evolution of wearable technology, several remarkable case studies have demonstrated the power of fashion-forward design in driving the widespread adoption and success of wearables. These trailblazing examples showcase how the integration of aesthetics and cutting-edge technology can create wearable devices that captivate users and transcend the boundaries of traditional tech gadgets.

- ❖ Apple Watch: One of the most iconic examples of a fashion-forward wearable is the Apple Watch. Launched in 2015, the Apple Watch quickly became a coveted accessory due to its sleek design, variety of interchangeable bands, and customizable watch faces. Apple's collaboration with high-end fashion brands, such as Hermès, further solidified the Apple Watch's position as a fashionable tech gadget. The device seamlessly blends into users' lifestyles, from fitness enthusiasts to business professionals, making it a quintessential example of successful fashion-tech fusion.

❖ Fitbit Versa: Fitbit, a pioneer in the fitness tracking industry, made significant strides in marrying fashion and functionality with the Fitbit Versa. This smartwatch boasts a slim and elegant design, offering users a wide range of stylish bands and watch faces to choose from. The Versa's focus on fashion appealed to a broader audience, not just fitness enthusiasts, positioning it as a versatile accessory that complements various lifestyles.

❖ Fossil Gen 5 Smartwatch: The Fossil Gen 5 Smartwatch stands out for its emphasis on classic watch design elements. Fossil's collaboration with renowned fashion brands, such as Michael Kors and

Emporio Armani, resulted in a line of smartwatches that cater to fashion-conscious consumers. The Gen 5 Smartwatch combines timeless aesthetics with advanced features like heart rate tracking, GPS, and Google's Wear OS, proving that wearables can be both sophisticated and tech-savvy.

❖ Ringly Smart Rings: Ringly redefined wearable tech with its smart rings, offering a stylish alternative to traditional smartwatches and fitness bands. These fashionable rings discreetly notify wearers of calls, messages, and other notifications through subtle vibrations and customizable light patterns. Ringly's focus on blending fashion with discreet tech features resonated with those seeking a seamless integration of technology into their everyday accessories.

❖ Snapchat Spectacles: Snapchat Spectacles broke new ground in the world of wearable tech by integrating a camera into a pair of stylish sunglasses. The Spectacles' playful design and trendy colors appealed to Snapchat's young and tech-savvy user base. By merging social media and fashion-forward eyewear,

Snapchat demonstrated how wearables can become a means of creative expression and social sharing.

These case studies illustrate how fashion-forward design can elevate wearables from gadgets to coveted accessories. By catering to users' diverse tastes and style preferences, these successful wearables have reshaped the perception of wearable technology, proving that aesthetics play a pivotal role in driving consumer adoption and enthusiasm. As more companies embrace the fusion of fashion and technology, wearables continue to evolve, offering an exciting future where style and innovation harmoniously coexist.

Chapter 3
Functionality and User Experience

A. Core Functionalities of Wearable Tech:

Wearable technology has evolved far beyond its initial simplistic origins, offering an impressive array of core functionalities that cater to various user needs. These functionalities form the backbone of wearables, transforming them from mere accessories to indispensable tools that enhance our daily lives.

* Health and Fitness Tracking: One of the fundamental functionalities of wearables is health and fitness tracking. Whether in the form of smartwatches, fitness bands, or smart rings, wearables can monitor a wide range of health metrics. From counting steps and tracking distance to measuring heart rate, sleep patterns, and even stress levels, wearables empower users to take control of their well-being and lead healthier lifestyles.

* Notifications and Communication: Wearables serve as extensions of our smartphones, providing timely

notifications and facilitating quick communication without the need to constantly check our phones. From incoming calls and text messages to social media alerts and calendar reminders, wearables keep us connected and informed on-the-go, ensuring we never miss important updates.

❖ Personalized Assistance: Advanced wearables leverage artificial intelligence and voice assistants to provide personalized assistance. These smart wearables can answer queries, set reminders, offer weather updates, and even control smart home devices, creating a seamless and hands-free user experience.

❖ Navigation and GPS: Wearables equipped with GPS capabilities are invaluable for navigation and location-based services. Whether walking, cycling, or driving, wearables with GPS help users find their way, explore new places, and stay on track during outdoor activities.

❖ Mobile Payments: Many modern wearables come with built-in NFC (Near Field Communication) technology, enabling mobile payments. With a simple tap, users can make secure transactions, eliminating the need to carry cash or cards.

❖ Music and Entertainment: Wearables with music playback functionality allow users to enjoy their favorite tunes on the go. Smartwatches, in particular, can control music playback on smartphones, making it convenient to switch tracks or adjust volume during workouts or daily commutes.

❖ Activity and Gesture Tracking: Some wearables incorporate sensors that can detect specific activities and gestures. For instance, wearables can recognize various exercises during workouts, detect hand movements for gesture-based controls, or even track specific movements for gaming applications.

❖ Environmental Monitoring: Certain wearables are equipped with environmental sensors to monitor air quality, temperature, UV exposure, and other environmental factors. These features can help users make informed decisions about their outdoor activities and well-being.

These core functionalities demonstrate the versatility of wearable technology and its potential to enrich our lives. By combining essential features with user-friendly interfaces and elegant designs, wearable tech has become an indispensable companion, enhancing productivity, promoting healthier lifestyles, and keeping us seamlessly connected in an increasingly digital world. As wearables continue to evolve, the scope of functionalities will likely expand, opening new horizons for how we interact with technology on a personal level.

B. User-Centered Design Approach:

In the realm of wearable technology, user experience reigns supreme. The user-centered design approach is at the core of creating wearables that not only boast impressive functionalities but also offer seamless interactions and intuitive experiences for users.

The user-centered design approach puts the end-users at the center of the design process. It involves understanding users' needs, preferences, and pain points to create wearables that truly cater to their lifestyles. This approach begins with in-depth research, including user interviews, surveys, and observations, to gain insights into the target audience's habits and expectations.

Empathy plays a crucial role in user-centered design. Designers and technologists empathize with users to put themselves in their shoes and truly understand their desires and frustrations. This empathetic understanding allows them to identify opportunities for innovation and craft solutions that address genuine user needs.

Prototyping is a key component of the user-centered design approach. Creating prototypes and mock-ups allows designers to gather feedback from users early in the development process. By iterating and refining the design based on user feedback, wearables can be tailored to meet users' expectations and preferences.

The user experience extends beyond functionality to encompass aesthetics, comfort, and ease of use. Designers strive to create wearables that are visually appealing, ergonomic, and feel like a natural extension of the user's body. Intuitive interfaces and straightforward interactions ensure that users can easily navigate through features without feeling overwhelmed or frustrated.

Usability testing is a critical aspect of user-centered design. Before launch, wearables undergo rigorous testing with real users to identify any usability issues or areas for improvement. This testing ensures that wearables perform as intended, providing a smooth and delightful experience for users.

Personalization is another key element of the user-centered design approach. Wearables offer customizable features and interfaces, allowing users to tailor the devices to suit their preferences and needs. Personalization enhances user satisfaction and fosters a sense of ownership over the wearable.

Accessibility is also prioritized in user-centered design. Designers consider the diverse needs of users, including those with disabilities, to ensure that wearables are inclusive and can be used by a wide range of individuals.

Ultimately, the user-centered design approach in wearable technology results in devices that resonate with users on a personal level. By prioritizing user experience, wearables become not only practical gadgets but also meaningful companions that seamlessly integrate into users' lives. This approach continues to drive the innovation and evolution of wearable tech, shaping a future where technology and humanity converge in a harmonious and user-centric manner.

C. Usability and Accessibility Considerations:

In the quest to create wearable technology that truly enhances users' lives, usability and accessibility stand as paramount considerations. Usability ensures that wearables are intuitive and easy to interact with, while accessibility ensures that these devices can be used by individuals with diverse needs and abilities.

Usability in wearable tech revolves around delivering a seamless and frustration-free experience for users. Designers strive to simplify complex interactions, minimize the learning curve, and streamline the user interface. Clear and straightforward navigation ensures that users can access features and functionalities effortlessly, regardless of their technological proficiency.

To achieve optimal usability, designers conduct extensive usability testing with real users. By observing how users interact with wearables, designers gain valuable insights into pain points and areas that require improvement. Iterative design processes are then employed to refine the user experience based on this feedback, leading to wearables that are both efficient and enjoyable to use.

Accessibility is an essential aspect of wearable tech design to ensure that all individuals, regardless of their abilities, can benefit from these devices. This consideration encompasses various aspects, including visual, auditory, motor, and cognitive accessibility.

Visual accessibility entails providing options for adjustable font sizes, high contrast interfaces, and color schemes suitable for individuals with visual impairments. Text-to-speech features and audio feedback enhance auditory accessibility, making wearables more inclusive for users with hearing difficulties.

Motor accessibility addresses the needs of users with limited dexterity or motor control. Wearables should have intuitive and adaptable controls that can be easily operated, even with limited physical capabilities. Voice commands and gesture-based interactions are examples of motor-accessible features.

Cognitive accessibility involves designing wearables with simplicity and clarity, reducing cognitive load for users with cognitive impairments. Consistent and predictable interfaces foster a sense of familiarity and ease of use, accommodating users with various cognitive abilities.

Furthermore, multilingual support and localization considerations contribute to the accessibility of wearables for users worldwide, irrespective of language barriers.

By implementing both usability and accessibility considerations, wearable tech transcends being exclusive gadgets for the tech-savvy and becomes a transformative force for a broader user base. It empowers users of all backgrounds, abilities, and ages to experience the benefits of wearables in their daily lives. The commitment to inclusive design ensures that wearable technology continues to break barriers, enhance communication, and foster independence, paving the way for a more connected and equitable future.

Chapter 4
Health and Fitness Wearables

A. Tracking Devices and Biometric Sensors:

Health and fitness wearables have emerged as a revolutionary category within the realm of wearable technology. These devices offer individuals valuable insights into their physical well-being, empowering them to take charge of their health and lead more active lifestyles. At the heart of these wearables are tracking devices and biometric sensors, which form the backbone of their health monitoring capabilities.

Tracking devices integrated into health and fitness wearables provide a comprehensive view of users' daily activities. Step counters, also known as pedometers, track the number of steps taken, encouraging users to achieve daily activity goals. Distance trackers calculate the total distance covered, enabling users to monitor their walking, running, or cycling progress.

Biometric sensors are instrumental in capturing and analyzing vital health data. Heart rate monitors measure the user's heart rate in real-time, providing valuable insights into cardiovascular health and intensity during workouts. Continuous heart rate tracking is especially beneficial for identifying potential health issues and optimizing fitness routines.

Sleep tracking is another vital functionality enabled by biometric sensors in health wearables. These sensors can monitor sleep patterns, duration, and the quality of sleep, helping users understand their sleep habits and make lifestyle adjustments to improve sleep quality.

Advanced health wearables incorporate SpO2 sensors to measure blood oxygen levels. SpO2 monitoring is particularly valuable during physical activities and for individuals with respiratory conditions, as it offers insights into oxygen saturation and overall respiratory health.

Blood pressure monitoring is also becoming prevalent in health wearables, providing users with the ability to monitor their blood pressure regularly and detect potential hypertension or anomalies.

Moreover, ECG (electrocardiogram) sensors are being integrated into some high-end health wearables. ECG capabilities allow users to record their heart's electrical activity, which can be crucial for identifying irregular heart rhythms and seeking medical attention if necessary.

By combining tracking devices and biometric sensors, health and fitness wearables empower users to track their progress, set and achieve health goals, and make informed decisions about their well-being. These devices serve as personal health assistants, offering data-driven insights and personalized recommendations, ultimately contributing to a healthier and more active lifestyle. As technology continues to advance, health wearables are expected to become even more sophisticated, revolutionizing the way we approach health management and preventive care.

B. Impact on Personal Health and Fitness Routines:

Health and fitness wearables have revolutionized the way individuals approach their personal well-being and exercise routines. The integration of these advanced devices into everyday life has had a profound impact on users, empowering them to make informed decisions about their health and fostering a more proactive approach to fitness.

One of the significant impacts of health and fitness wearables is the increased awareness of physical activity levels. By continuously tracking steps, distance, and calories burned, wearables provide users with a real-time view of their daily activity. This awareness motivates users to be more active and make conscious efforts to achieve their fitness goals, such as reaching a certain step count or increasing daily exercise duration.

The ability to monitor heart rate during workouts and daily activities has also transformed fitness routines. Wearables offer insights into exercise intensity, allowing users to optimize their workouts and train within specific heart rate zones for more effective results. This data-driven approach to fitness enables users to make data-backed decisions, leading to better performance and enhanced overall fitness.

Sleep tracking is another game-changer in the realm of health wearables. By analyzing sleep patterns and quality, users gain a deeper understanding of their sleep habits and potential sleep-related issues. Armed with this information, individuals can make lifestyle changes to improve sleep hygiene and overall well-being.

Health and fitness wearables also encourage a sense of community and healthy competition. Many wearables offer social features that allow users to connect with friends and family, share achievements, and engage in friendly challenges. This sense of community fosters accountability and motivation, as users support and inspire one another on their fitness journeys.

Furthermore, wearables have a positive impact on preventive health care. Regular monitoring of biometric data, such as heart rate and blood pressure, can aid in early detection of potential health issues. Early warnings provided by wearables empower users to seek medical attention promptly, helping to prevent more serious health complications.

The personalized feedback and data-driven insights provided by health and fitness wearables also promote behavior change. Users can set realistic health goals and receive feedback based on their progress, leading to a sense of accomplishment and motivation to continue making positive lifestyle choices.

In conclusion, health and fitness wearables have transformed personal health management and fitness routines. By offering real-time data, personalized insights, and a sense of community, wearables empower users to take a proactive role in their well-being. As these devices continue to advance, they will play an increasingly vital role in preventive health care and inspire individuals worldwide to embrace a healthier and more active lifestyle.

C. Potential Future Advancements in Health Wearables:

The future of health wearables holds immense promise, as technology continues to advance and innovators push the boundaries of what is possible. These potential advancements have the potential to transform the landscape of personal health management and preventive care, further empowering individuals to lead healthier lives.

- ❖ Continuous Health Monitoring: Future health wearables are expected to provide even more comprehensive and continuous health monitoring. Advancements in sensor technology may enable wearables to monitor a broader range of health metrics, including glucose levels for diabetics, hydration levels, and even specific biomarkers for early detection of diseases.

- ❖ Artificial Intelligence and Predictive Analysis: The integration of artificial intelligence (AI) into health wearables will revolutionize data analysis and insights. AI algorithms can process vast amounts of biometric data, identifying patterns and trends that may go unnoticed by traditional means. This could lead to predictive analysis, alerting users to potential health risks and providing personalized recommendations for preventive actions.

❖ Non-Invasive Health Monitoring: Future health wearables may focus on non-invasive monitoring, reducing the need for pricking or invasive procedures. Wearables that use optical sensors to measure blood pressure, blood glucose levels, and other vital health indicators could offer a more comfortable and user-friendly experience.

❖ Environmental and Contextual Sensing: Health wearables may incorporate environmental and contextual sensing to offer a more holistic view of users' health. Wearables equipped with pollution sensors, UV monitoring, and activity context recognition can provide users with insights into how their environment and activities impact their well-being.

❖ Integration of Healthcare Ecosystems: Future health wearables may seamlessly integrate with healthcare ecosystems, allowing for secure data sharing with medical professionals. This integration can facilitate remote patient monitoring and enable healthcare providers to offer more personalized and timely interventions.

❖ Augmented Reality (AR) for Medical Visualization: AR technology integrated into health wearables could enhance medical visualization and diagnostics. Wearables with AR capabilities could overlay medical imaging or vital health data directly onto the user's view, aiding medical professionals in diagnostics and treatment planning.

❖ Smart Drug Delivery Systems: Advanced health wearables may incorporate smart drug delivery systems, enabling the precise and timely administration of medications based on real-time health data. Such wearables could be invaluable for individuals managing chronic conditions or undergoing specific treatments.

❖ Integration with Digital Therapeutics: Future health wearables could work in tandem with digital therapeutics, offering personalized interventions and treatment plans for various health conditions. These wearables could provide real-time coaching, behavior change support, and therapeutic activities to optimize health outcomes.

In conclusion, the potential future advancements in health wearables are incredibly promising, heralding a new era of personalized and proactive health management. As technology continues to evolve, these wearables will become even more sophisticated, transforming the way individuals monitor and optimize their health. The fusion of advanced sensors, artificial intelligence, and seamless integration with healthcare ecosystems will empower users to make more informed decisions about their well-being, ultimately leading to healthier and happier lives.

Chapter 5
Smart Fashion and Interactive Clothing

A. Integration of Technology into Clothing:

The intersection of technology and fashion has given rise to the exciting realm of smart fashion and interactive clothing. Designers and technologists are collaborating to seamlessly integrate technology into garments, transforming them into functional and interactive wearables.

One of the key elements of this integration is the use of smart fabrics and textiles. These innovative materials are embedded with conductive threads, sensors, and microelectronics that can detect and respond to various stimuli. Smart fabrics open up a world of possibilities, allowing clothing to interact with the wearer and the environment.

For instance, temperature-sensitive fabrics can adapt to changes in weather, providing warmth in cold conditions and cooling effects in hot weather. Similarly, moisture-wicking fabrics keep the wearer dry and comfortable during physical activities.

Interactive clothing can be equipped with touch-sensitive areas that respond to gestures or touches, enabling wearers to control devices or access information without the need for physical buttons or screens. This touch-enabled functionality enhances convenience and safety, particularly for users engaged in activities where hands-free interaction is crucial.

Light-emitting fabrics and LED elements are also used in smart fashion, creating stunning visual effects and enhancing visibility in low-light conditions. These elements can be incorporated into clothing, making them not only fashionable but also practical for night-time or outdoor activities.

Moreover, smart fashion includes wearables with biometric sensors woven into the fabric. These sensors can measure heart rate, respiratory rate, and other vital signs, providing real-time health monitoring without the need for additional gadgets.

The integration of technology also extends to the realm of augmented reality (AR) and virtual reality (VR). Clothing can be designed with AR markers or interactive surfaces that trigger virtual experiences when viewed through AR-enabled devices. This fusion of fashion and immersive technology offers new ways for users to interact with digital content in the physical world.

The possibilities for technology integration in clothing seem boundless. As designers and technologists continue to innovate, we can expect to see even more sophisticated and practical applications of smart fashion and interactive clothing. This convergence of fashion and technology not only enhances the aesthetics of clothing but also transforms garments into tools that enrich our daily lives, offering a glimpse into the exciting future of wearable technology.

B. Reactive and Responsive Garments:

In the fascinating world of smart fashion and interactive clothing, reactive and responsive garments take center stage. These innovative wearables go beyond mere aesthetics, transforming into dynamic companions that adapt and respond to the wearer's needs and the surrounding environment.

Reactive garments are designed to respond to external stimuli, triggering specific reactions based on changes in the environment. For example, reactive clothing with color-changing properties can adjust its hues in response to temperature variations or ambient light conditions. This not only adds an artistic touch to fashion but also serves as a practical indicator of environmental changes.

Another application of reactive garments involves responsive elements that interact with the wearer's movements or biometric data. Clothing with motion-sensitive LEDs or sound-reactive fabrics can create mesmerizing visual and auditory effects that synchronize with the wearer's actions. These garments blur the boundaries between fashion and performance art, immersing the wearer in a dynamic and captivating experience.

Furthermore, responsive garments can enhance safety and comfort. For instance, clothing with built-in sensors can detect body posture and adjust its fit to optimize ergonomics and prevent discomfort during physical activities. Responsive garments can also analyze sweat or body temperature to regulate ventilation, ensuring the wearer remains cool during intense workouts.

Some responsive garments integrate haptic feedback, which uses tactile sensations to communicate information. For instance, haptic feedback in clothing can guide wearers with vibrations or pressure patterns, serving as a navigation aid for individuals with visual impairments or assisting in learning complex motor skills.

Reactive and responsive garments extend the boundaries of wearable technology, offering wearers a dynamic and immersive experience. The integration of smart fabrics, sensors, and microelectronics enables fashion to become an interactive medium, fostering a deeper connection between the wearer and their clothing.

As technology continues to advance, the potential for reactive and responsive garments grows exponentially. These interactive wearables provide a glimpse into the future of fashion, where clothing becomes a dynamic canvas for artistic expression, a source of valuable information, and a means of enhancing daily experiences. The combination of technology and fashion brings forth a new era of self-expression and practical functionality, paving the way for a transformative future of smart fashion and interactive clothing.

C. Novel Applications of Smart Fashion in Various Industries:

The world of smart fashion and interactive clothing transcends the realm of style and self-expression, finding novel applications in a wide range of industries. The seamless integration of technology into garments has opened up new possibilities, revolutionizing the way we interact with clothing and enhancing various sectors in innovative ways.

❖ Healthcare: Smart fashion has made significant strides in the healthcare industry. Garments embedded with biometric sensors can monitor patients' vital signs continuously, providing valuable data for remote patient monitoring. These wearables offer insights into patient health, enabling healthcare professionals to detect early signs of health issues and tailor personalized treatment plans.

❖ Sports and Fitness: In the sports and fitness industry, smart fashion is redefining the way athletes train and compete. Motion-sensitive garments can analyze athletes' movements, offering real-time feedback to optimize performance and prevent injuries. Additionally, wearables with biometric sensors help athletes monitor their heart rate, recovery time, and hydration levels, leading to better training outcomes.

❖ Entertainment and Performances: Smart fashion has become an integral part of entertainment and performance events. Performers don interactive garments with responsive elements, creating visually captivating and immersive experiences for the audience. These garments synchronize with music, lights, and choreography, transforming live shows into multisensory spectacles.

❖ Gaming and Virtual Reality (VR): In the gaming industry, smart fashion is elevating the immersive experience. Reactive clothing can respond to in-game events, such as changing colors to reflect a character's health status. Wearables with haptic feedback enhance VR experiences, making virtual interactions more realistic and engaging for gamers.

❖ Fashion Tech Retail: Smart fashion has found a place in the retail industry, with connected garments enhancing the shopping experience. Virtual try-on applications allow customers to visualize how clothing fits and looks on them before making a purchase. Smart mirrors in fitting rooms can display additional product information and suggest complementary items, elevating the overall shopping journey.

❖ Military and Security: In the military and security sectors, smart fashion contributes to enhanced performance and safety. Wearables with integrated GPS and environmental sensors aid soldiers in navigation and provide situational awareness in challenging terrains. Smart textiles with biometric monitoring can detect signs of fatigue or stress, alerting personnel to potential risks.

❖ Environmental and Industrial Applications: Smart fashion has potential applications in environmental monitoring and industrial safety. Wearables with pollution sensors can detect air quality, enabling individuals to make informed decisions about outdoor activities. In industrial settings, smart garments equipped with proximity sensors can enhance worker safety by alerting them to potential hazards.

The novel applications of smart fashion continue to expand, demonstrating the versatility and transformative potential of technology-integrated clothing. As technology advances, smart fashion will undoubtedly play an even more significant role in shaping various industries, enriching experiences, and redefining the boundaries of what clothing can accomplish.

Chapter 6
Wearable Tech in Entertainment and Gaming

A. Immersive Experiences and Augmented Reality:

Wearable technology has ushered in a new era of immersive experiences and augmented reality (AR) in the realm of entertainment and gaming. These cutting-edge wearables have transformed how users interact with digital content, blurring the lines between the real world and the virtual realm.

AR wearables, such as smart glasses and headsets, have revolutionized the way we experience entertainment. By overlaying digital information onto the physical environment, these wearables enhance storytelling and gaming experiences like never before. From interactive storytelling in theme parks to location-based AR games in urban environments, AR wearables offer unparalleled levels of immersion.

In the gaming industry, wearable AR devices have taken gameplay to extraordinary heights. Gamers can step into alternate realities, where virtual objects blend seamlessly with the real world. Through AR wearables, users can battle digital monsters in their living rooms, solve puzzles in city streets, or compete in sports challenges within their surroundings.

Moreover, AR wearables have transformed live events and performances. Attendees at concerts, festivals, and sports events can enjoy enhanced experiences with real-time AR elements projected onto their wearable devices. AR wearables enable performers to interact with the audience in new and engaging ways, creating unforgettable moments that transcend traditional entertainment boundaries.

Additionally, wearable tech has brought multi-user AR experiences to the forefront. Multiple users equipped with AR wearables can engage in shared digital adventures, collaboratively exploring virtual worlds or playing interactive AR games together. This social aspect of wearable AR fosters a sense of camaraderie and shared excitement among users.

In the world of entertainment, smart glasses and headsets offer personalized viewing experiences. Wearers can enjoy immersive cinematic experiences from the comfort of their eyewear, making movie-watching a more private and dynamic activity.

Wearable tech also enables practical applications in cultural experiences and museum tours. AR wearables can provide historical context, overlaying virtual exhibits and information on real artifacts, enriching visitors' understanding and engagement.

The potential for immersive experiences and AR wearables seems boundless. As technology advances, wearables are likely to become even more sophisticated, offering interactive experiences that captivate and enthrall users. The fusion of wearable tech and entertainment has unlocked new realms of creativity, redefining how we consume content and paving the way for a future where virtual and physical realities intertwine seamlessly.

B. Gamification of Wearables:

The gamification of wearables has emerged as a compelling trend, blending elements of gaming and interactive experiences into everyday activities. This innovative approach has transformed wearables into more than just functional gadgets, infusing them with elements of fun, challenge, and motivation.

Gamification strategies encourage users to engage with their wearables by introducing game-like features and mechanics. These elements appeal to users' intrinsic desire for achievement, competition, and rewards, turning ordinary tasks into enjoyable and rewarding experiences.

One of the key aspects of gamification is the use of achievement systems. Wearables set goals and challenges for users to complete, such as reaching a specific step count, maintaining consistent exercise routines, or achieving a certain heart rate target during workouts. When users accomplish these goals, they are rewarded with badges, points, or virtual rewards, fostering a sense of accomplishment and encouraging continued engagement.

Leaderboards are another gamification element that promotes friendly competition. Wearables allow users to compare their achievements with those of friends or a broader community. The competitive spirit motivates users to push their limits, striving to rank higher on leaderboards and outperform their peers.

Incorporating storytelling into wearables is another gamification tactic. Wearables with interactive narratives or quest-like challenges create a more immersive and engaging experience. Users embark on adventures, solve puzzles, and unlock new content as they progress through the story, making wearables a platform for interactive storytelling and entertainment.

Virtual rewards and incentives are powerful tools in gamifying wearables. Users can earn virtual currency, unlock special features, or access exclusive content as they achieve milestones or complete challenges. These rewards provide a sense of progress and a tangible return on their efforts, reinforcing positive behavior.

Social engagement plays a significant role in the gamification of wearables. Wearable apps often incorporate social sharing features, allowing users to share their achievements, challenges, and progress with friends and social networks. The social aspect fosters a sense of community, encouraging support and encouragement among users.

Gamification has proven to be an effective strategy in motivating users to adopt healthier lifestyles and maintain consistent habits. By infusing wearables with elements of play and challenge, users are more likely to stay engaged, set and achieve goals, and experience a sense of enjoyment while using their devices.

As wearable technology continues to evolve, the gamification trend is expected to grow, offering exciting possibilities for enhancing user engagement, personal development, and entertainment. The convergence of wearable tech and gamification opens up new frontiers in making health and fitness endeavors enjoyable, fostering a more connected and motivated user community.

C. Entertainment Applications and Implications:

Wearable technology has revolutionized the entertainment industry, introducing groundbreaking applications that elevate the way we experience content and interact with digital experiences. These wearables offer an array of exciting entertainment applications and carry significant implications for the future of immersive experiences.

❖ Virtual Reality (VR) Experiences: Wearable VR headsets have become a game-changer in the entertainment world. By immersing users in virtual environments, VR wearables offer captivating experiences in gaming, storytelling, and interactive simulations. Users can explore new worlds, participate in thrilling adventures, and interact with digital elements in a way that feels incredibly real.

❖ Augmented Reality (AR) Entertainment: AR wearables blend virtual elements with the real world, opening up unique entertainment opportunities. From AR games that bring virtual characters into the physical environment to AR-enhanced performances and art installations, wearables enable users to experience a rich fusion of digital and physical realms.

❖ Enhanced Live Events: Wearable tech has transformed live events, such as concerts and sports games. Attendees equipped with smart glasses or AR headsets can access real-time information, view interactive content, and enjoy personalized experiences that complement the live performances, enhancing their overall enjoyment.

❖ Interactive Storytelling: Wearables have introduced new dimensions to storytelling. AR and smart glasses allow readers to immerse themselves in interactive narratives, where characters and plots come to life in the physical world. Interactive storytelling empowers users to become active participants in the stories they read or watch.

❖ Location-Based Entertainment: AR wearables have enabled location-based entertainment experiences. Users can engage in AR-based treasure hunts, solve puzzles in real-world settings, or participate in interactive city tours, providing a novel and dynamic way to explore and interact with the world around them.

❖ Social VR and AR: Wearables have fostered a sense of social connectedness in virtual environments. Users can gather in virtual spaces through their wearables, interacting with friends, colleagues, or even strangers from across the globe, transcending physical barriers and creating meaningful social experiences.

❖ Privacy and Ethical Considerations: As entertainment wearables become more prevalent, privacy and ethical considerations come to the forefront. The collection of personal data, tracking of user behavior, and potential impact on mental health raise important questions regarding user consent and responsible design.

❖ Enhanced User Engagement: Entertainment wearables offer a level of engagement that traditional media cannot match. Users become active participants rather than passive consumers, leading to more profound emotional connections with the content and a higher level of user satisfaction.

As entertainment wearables continue to evolve, the possibilities for enriching the entertainment landscape are limitless. From transforming the way we consume content to enhancing social interactions and storytelling, wearables have introduced a new dimension of engagement and interactivity. However, the responsible implementation of wearable tech requires ongoing consideration of user privacy and well-being, ensuring that these technologies serve to enrich lives while respecting individual rights and values.

Chapter 7
The Role of AI and Data in Wearable Tech

A. AI-Driven Wearables and Personalization:

Artificial Intelligence (AI) plays a pivotal role in shaping the future of wearable technology, driving innovation, and enhancing user experiences. AI-driven wearables have the capability to learn from user data, adapt to individual preferences, and offer personalized insights and recommendations.

The integration of AI allows wearables to process vast amounts of data generated by sensors and user interactions. AI algorithms analyze this data, identifying patterns, and gaining deep insights into user behavior, health metrics, and lifestyle habits. This data-driven approach enables wearables to understand users on a profound level, offering personalized experiences tailored to each individual's needs.

One of the key aspects of AI-driven wearables is personalization. These wearables can create a customized user profile based on historical data, preferences, and goals. From fitness trackers to smartwatches, wearables can analyze user patterns and offer personalized fitness goals, wellness recommendations, and lifestyle adjustments.

For example, a fitness wearable powered by AI can assess an individual's exercise routine, heart rate trends, and sleep patterns to design a personalized fitness plan. This plan may include specific workout routines, nutrition guidance, and sleep optimization strategies based on the user's unique requirements.

AI-driven wearables can also provide real-time coaching and feedback. Wearables equipped with voice assistants can offer personalized guidance during workouts, reminding users to maintain proper form, encouraging them to reach their goals, and offering motivational messages based on individual progress.

Moreover, AI-driven wearables excel in predictive analysis. By continuously monitoring data and identifying trends, wearables can anticipate user needs and provide timely recommendations. For instance, wearables can predict potential health issues based on biometric data, prompting users to seek medical attention proactively.

The integration of AI also enables wearables to learn from user interactions. Wearables can adapt and refine their recommendations based on user feedback and responses. This iterative learning process ensures that wearables continuously improve in providing personalized and relevant content.

However, with the power of AI and data collection comes the responsibility to ensure user privacy and data security. Manufacturers must prioritize robust data protection measures and transparent data usage policies to instill user trust in AI-driven wearables.

As technology continues to advance, AI-driven wearables will become increasingly sophisticated, offering users a truly personalized and intelligent experience. By harnessing the power of AI and data analytics, wearables have the potential to transform health management, enhance lifestyle choices, and empower individuals to lead healthier, more fulfilling lives.

B. Data Privacy and Security Challenges:

While the integration of AI and data in wearable tech holds tremendous promise, it also presents significant challenges related to data privacy and security. Wearable devices collect a vast amount of personal data, ranging from health and fitness metrics to location information and user behavior. Protecting this data from unauthorized access and ensuring user privacy have become critical concerns in the wearable tech industry.

❖ Data Breaches and Cybersecurity Risks: Wearable devices store sensitive user data, including health records, biometric information, and location history. A data breach or cybersecurity incident can have severe consequences, leading to identity theft, fraud, and compromised personal information. Manufacturers and developers must implement robust security measures to safeguard against cyber threats and potential data breaches.

❖ Inadequate Data Encryption: Data transmitted between wearable devices and companion apps or cloud servers must be encrypted to prevent interception by malicious actors. Weak or inadequate data encryption can expose user data to potential breaches, making encryption protocols and encryption key management essential components of data security.

❖ User Consent and Transparency: AI-driven wearables often rely on extensive data collection to provide personalized insights and recommendations. However, users must be fully informed about the data being collected, how it will be used, and who will have access to it. Manufacturers must prioritize transparency and obtain explicit user consent before collecting and utilizing personal data.

❖ Third-Party Data Sharing: Wearable tech companies may collaborate with third-party entities, such as healthcare providers, insurance companies, or advertisers. Data sharing with these parties can raise privacy concerns if not properly regulated. Companies should establish clear data sharing policies and ensure that user data is not used for purposes beyond what users have consented to.

❖ Anonymization and De-identification: AI algorithms often require large datasets for training and optimization. Anonymization and de-identification techniques are used to protect user privacy during data processing. However, it is challenging to guarantee complete anonymization, and there is always a risk of re-identification if data is mishandled.

❖ Cross-Device Data Integration: Wearable devices often communicate with other smart devices, creating opportunities for cross-device data integration. While this integration can enhance user experiences, it also raises concerns about data aggregation and user profiling, potentially leading to invasive tracking of users' activities and habits.

❖ User Empowerment and Data Ownership: Wearable tech users should have the right to access, review, and delete their data at any time. Companies should provide user-friendly interfaces for managing data preferences and should respect users' rights to ownership and control over their personal information.

Addressing these data privacy and security challenges is essential to ensure that wearable technology can be used responsibly and ethically. As wearables become more integrated into our daily lives, user trust and confidence in the security of their data become fundamental factors in the widespread adoption of wearable tech and the realization of its transformative potential.

C. Ethical Considerations in Wearable Tech Development:

As wearable technology continues to advance, developers and manufacturers must grapple with various ethical considerations to ensure that these devices are designed and utilized responsibly, respecting user rights and societal values. Ethical implications in wearable tech development encompass a broad spectrum of concerns, ranging from data privacy and consent to fairness and inclusivity in AI algorithms.

❖ Data Privacy and Informed Consent: Data collected by wearable devices often contains sensitive information about users' health, behavior, and location. It is imperative for developers to prioritize data privacy, implementing robust security measures to protect user data from unauthorized access or breaches. Transparent and informed consent procedures must be in place, ensuring that users are fully aware of the data collected, its purpose, and how it will be used.

❖ Bias and Fairness in AI Algorithms: AI-driven wearables rely on algorithms to process user data and provide personalized insights. Developers must be vigilant about identifying and mitigating bias in these algorithms to ensure fair and equitable outcomes. Biased algorithms could perpetuate discriminatory practices or reinforce stereotypes, leading to harmful consequences for certain user groups.

❖ Inclusivity and Accessibility: Wearable tech should be designed with inclusivity and accessibility in mind. Developers must consider the needs of users with disabilities, ensuring that wearable devices and companion apps are usable and beneficial to a diverse range of individuals. This includes features like voice control, text-to-speech, and compatibility with assistive technologies.

❖ Health and Psychological Impact: Wearable tech that tracks and analyzes health metrics can have both positive and negative impacts on users' well-being. Developers must be aware of the potential psychological effects of continuous health monitoring and ensure that data insights are presented responsibly, avoiding unnecessary alarm or anxiety.

❖ End-of-Life and Sustainability: The lifespan of wearable devices is a critical ethical consideration. Manufacturers should promote sustainability by designing products with easily replaceable parts and recycling programs. Discarded wearables could contain sensitive user data, necessitating secure data erasure procedures to protect user privacy.

❖ Children and Vulnerable Users: Extra care must be taken when developing wearables for children and vulnerable populations. Data collection and processing involving minors require special considerations, including parental consent and strict privacy safeguards. Wearable tech for vulnerable users should prioritize user safety and well-being.

❖ Transparency and Explainability: AI-driven wearables often make decisions based on complex algorithms. Developers must prioritize transparency and explainability, ensuring that users can understand how decisions are made and why specific recommendations are provided. Transparent AI fosters user trust and empowers users to make informed choices.

❖ Impact on Social Behavior: Wearable tech can influence social interactions and behavior. Ethical considerations should be given to potential negative consequences of wearable use, such as excessive screen time or detachment from real-world experiences. Responsible design should encourage healthy and balanced use of wearables.

❖ Accountability and Regulation: Developers and manufacturers must be accountable for the ethical implications of their wearable products. Industry-wide best practices, ethical guidelines, and independent oversight can help ensure that wearable tech adheres to ethical standards and avoids unethical practices.

In conclusion, ethical considerations are integral to the development and deployment of wearable technology. By prioritizing data privacy, fairness in AI algorithms, inclusivity, and user well-being, developers can create wearable tech that enhances lives while respecting user rights and societal values. Ethical practices in wearable tech development are crucial for building trust with users and fostering responsible technological advancements.

Chapter 8
Challenges and Future Prospects

A. Battery Life and Energy Efficiency:

Battery life and energy efficiency remain significant challenges in the development and adoption of wearable technology. As wearables continue to offer more advanced features and capabilities, the demand for power increases, putting strain on the already limited battery capacities of these compact devices.

One of the primary concerns for users of wearable tech is the need for frequent charging. While smartphone users have grown accustomed to daily charging routines, wearables often require charging every few days or even more frequently, depending on usage. This frequent need for charging can be inconvenient, especially for users who rely on wearables for continuous health monitoring or other critical functions.

To address this challenge, wearable manufacturers are constantly striving to improve battery efficiency and develop new battery technologies. Research focuses on finding alternative power sources, such as flexible and stretchable batteries, energy harvesting mechanisms from body movement or solar power, and even biofuel cells that harness energy from the wearer's sweat.

Energy efficiency is another critical aspect of wearable tech development. Efficient power management is essential to extend battery life and optimize the overall performance of wearables. Device firmware and software play a significant role in ensuring that the wearable operates efficiently, avoiding unnecessary background processes that drain battery power.

Advanced power-saving modes and adaptive algorithms are being integrated into wearables to optimize energy consumption. For instance, wearables can adjust display brightness based on ambient light conditions or activate power-saving mode when the device is not in active use.

Moreover, developers are exploring ways to reduce the power consumption of sensors and components without compromising functionality. For example, using low-power Bluetooth connectivity, employing energy-efficient processors, and optimizing sensor sampling rates can help minimize energy consumption.

Furthermore, wearable tech is increasingly adopting ultra-low-power microcontrollers and system-on-chip (SoC) designs. These specialized chips are designed to handle specific tasks efficiently, consuming minimal power during operation.

In the future, advancements in battery technology and energy efficiency are expected to play a crucial role in overcoming the challenges faced by wearable tech. Innovative developments like self-charging or energy-scavenging materials could lead to wearables that never need external charging. Additionally, breakthroughs in materials science may pave the way for higher-capacity and longer-lasting batteries in smaller form factors.

Standardization and regulation of energy efficiency norms in wearable tech could also lead to more consistent performance across devices. Industry collaborations and benchmarks could drive the adoption of best practices in power management, benefiting both manufacturers and consumers.

Overall, while battery life and energy efficiency are significant challenges in the current landscape of wearable technology, ongoing research and innovation are promising signs for the future. As wearables become more integral to our lives, advancements in battery technology and energy efficiency will play a crucial role in making wearable tech more practical, convenient, and seamlessly integrated into our daily routines.

B. Social Acceptance and Cultural Impact:

As wearable technology becomes more prevalent, social acceptance and its cultural impact are significant factors that influence the adoption and integration of wearables into society. The design, appearance, and perceived benefits of wearables can either foster enthusiasm or resistance among potential users, making it crucial for developers and manufacturers to consider social and cultural contexts.

One of the key challenges for wearables is achieving a balance between functionality and aesthetics. The design of wearables plays a pivotal role in their acceptance among users. While some users prioritize the practicality and functionality of wearables, others place equal importance on their appearance and style. To achieve broad social acceptance, wearables need to seamlessly blend into everyday fashion choices and reflect diverse cultural preferences.

Cultural considerations also play a vital role in the adoption of wearables across different regions and communities. Wearables that resonate with the cultural values and norms of specific societies are more likely to be embraced. For example, in some cultures, wearing technology on the body might be perceived as intrusive or a violation of personal space, while in others, it may be seen as a status symbol or a symbol of progress.

Privacy concerns are closely tied to social acceptance. As wearables gather and process personal data, individuals may feel uncomfortable with the idea of constant monitoring and data sharing. Developers must prioritize user privacy and implement features that allow users to control the data they share and the visibility of their wearable tech activities.

Moreover, the cultural impact of wearables extends beyond individual users to societal norms and behavior. Wearable technology can influence social interactions and etiquettes. For example, the use of smartwatches and smart glasses during conversations or social events may raise questions about distraction and attentiveness. Establishing acceptable wearable tech practices within social contexts is an ongoing challenge.

Cultural perceptions of wearables can also impact their applications in various industries. In some professional settings, wearables may be embraced as tools that enhance productivity and safety, while in others, they may raise concerns about surveillance and intrusion into personal space.

To address the challenges related to social acceptance and cultural impact, collaborative efforts are needed. Developers, designers, and sociologists can work together to create wearables that respect cultural sensitivities and foster positive interactions. User feedback and participatory design processes can help ensure that wearables align with the needs and preferences of diverse user groups.

As wearables become more integrated into daily life, cultural norms and social acceptance will continue to evolve. Public awareness campaigns and educational initiatives can play a vital role in promoting the responsible and ethical use of wearable tech. By addressing social acceptance and cultural impact proactively, wearable technology has the potential to become a more inclusive and transformative force in enhancing the way we interact with technology and each other.

C. Predictions for the Future of Wearable Technology:

Wearable technology has come a long way since its inception, and its future holds tremendous potential for innovation and transformation. As technology continues to evolve, several predictions emerge for the future of wearable tech, shaping how we interact with devices and how wearables integrate into our daily lives.

❖ Seamless Integration and Invisible Wearables: In the future, wearables are expected to become more seamlessly integrated into our clothing and accessories. Invisible wearables, such as smart fabrics and biometric sensors embedded in clothing, will become more prevalent, providing discreet monitoring and functionality without compromising aesthetics.

❖ Health Monitoring and Preventive Care: Wearable health devices are poised to become even more advanced, providing comprehensive health monitoring and early disease detection. Advanced sensors and AI algorithms will offer real-time health insights, empowering users to take proactive measures for preventive care.

❖ Brain-Computer Interfaces (BCIs): The development of BCIs will revolutionize wearable tech. BCIs will enable direct communication between the human brain and external devices, allowing users to control wearables through their thoughts and perform tasks without physical interaction.

❖ Augmented Reality (AR) Contact Lenses: Advancements in miniaturization and display technologies may lead to AR contact lenses that overlay digital information onto the wearer's field of view. AR lenses will offer enhanced user experiences without the need for bulky headsets.

❖ Personalized AI Companions: AI-driven virtual assistants will evolve into personalized companions that understand users on a deeper level. These AI companions will offer emotional support, personalized recommendations, and adapt to users' preferences and moods.

❖ Wearables for Mental Health: Wearable tech will play a significant role in mental health management. Devices capable of monitoring stress levels, emotional states, and sleep patterns will provide valuable insights and interventions to support mental well-being.

❖ Energy Harvesting and Self-Charging Wearables: Energy-efficient wearables will incorporate energy-harvesting technologies, enabling self-charging through body movements or ambient sources. This innovation will reduce the dependency on traditional batteries and enhance the sustainability of wearables.

❖ Wearables in Extended Reality (XR): Wearable tech will integrate with extended reality (XR) experiences, blurring the lines between the physical and virtual worlds. XR wearables will offer immersive interactions in augmented, virtual, and mixed reality environments.

❖ Wearable Ecosystem Integration: Wearable devices will become more interconnected, creating a seamless ecosystem where wearables interact with smartphones, smart home devices, and other IoT devices. This integration will lead to more personalized and context-aware user experiences.

❖ Ethical AI and Data Governance: As wearable tech gains prominence, ethical considerations will be prioritized in AI algorithms and data governance. Transparent data practices, user control over data, and accountability will be essential in building trust with users.

In conclusion, the future of wearable technology is promising and transformative. Advancements in materials science, AI, energy efficiency, and user-centric design will shape wearables into indispensable companions that seamlessly enhance our lives. The integration of wearables into diverse industries, such as healthcare, entertainment, and fitness, will drive innovation and open up new possibilities for personalization and user experiences. As technology continues to advance, wearable tech's future is bound to bring about exciting developments that redefine how we interact with technology and enrich our daily experiences.

Conclusion

A. Recap of Key Points:

The journey through the world of wearable technology has revealed the convergence of fashion and functionality, resulting in a technology revolution that is transforming how we interact with digital information and our surroundings. In this book, "Wearable Tech: Fashion Meets Functionality," we explored the evolution of wearables, the integration of fashion and technology, and the myriad of ways wearables have impacted our lives.

The introduction delved into the rise of wearable technology, highlighting its rapid growth and adoption across various sectors. We explored how the intersection of fashion and functionality has given rise to wearables that not only deliver cutting-edge features but also appeal to personal style preferences, making wearables more accessible and appealing to a wider audience.

The purpose and scope of this book were to examine the historical background of wearable technology and its early attempts and inventions. We learned about the significant technological advancements that paved the way for modern wearables, turning them from novelty gadgets into indispensable tools for health monitoring, productivity enhancement, and entertainment.

The role of aesthetics in wearable tech was discussed, emphasizing the importance of design and how it has influenced the adoption of wearables. The integration of fashion designers and technologists has led to the emergence of fashion-forward wearables that blur the line between technology and fashion.

We also explored case studies of successful fashion-forward wearables, exemplifying how innovative designs and user-centric approaches have led to commercial success and user satisfaction.

The functional aspect of wearables was analyzed in-depth, uncovering core functionalities and user experiences. We discussed the significance of a user-centered design approach to create wearables that seamlessly fit into users' lives and address their specific needs.

Usability and accessibility considerations were explored, acknowledging the importance of making wearables inclusive and user-friendly for individuals of all abilities and backgrounds.

The book then dived into specific categories of wearables, such as health and fitness wearables, and their impact on personal health and fitness routines. We explored the potential future advancements in health wearables, providing insights into how wearables will continue to revolutionize healthcare.

The chapters on smart fashion and interactive clothing elucidated the integration of technology into clothing, paving the way for reactive and responsive garments that redefine the concept of fashion and self-expression.

We also examined the realm of entertainment and gaming, where wearable tech has ushered in immersive experiences and augmented reality. Gamification of wearables and its implications for user engagement and motivation were explored, showcasing the exciting possibilities that lie ahead in entertainment and gaming.

The role of AI and data in wearables brought attention to the personalized experiences and challenges related to data privacy and security. Ethical considerations in wearable tech development highlighted the importance of user empowerment, data ownership, and cultural sensitivity.

Finally, we gazed into the future of wearable technology, predicting seamless integration, advanced health monitoring, and the emergence of brain-computer interfaces. We envisaged wearable tech transforming mental health management, leveraging energy-harvesting technologies, and creating interconnected ecosystems.

In conclusion, wearable technology has transcended its early iterations to become a pivotal force in our daily lives. By striking a harmonious balance between fashion and functionality, wearables have become enablers of personal expression, health optimization, and immersive experiences. However, as wearables continue to evolve, we must address ethical, privacy, and energy challenges to ensure that wearable tech enhances our lives responsibly and ethically. The future of wearable technology is bright, promising novel opportunities and possibilities that will reshape how we perceive, interact, and benefit from technology in our ever-evolving world.

B. Closing Thoughts on the Fusion of Fashion and Functionality:

As we conclude our exploration of wearable technology and its remarkable fusion of fashion and functionality, we are left with a profound appreciation for the transformative power of this dynamic intersection. Wearable tech has evolved from mere gadgets into integral components of our daily lives, seamlessly integrating technology with personal style, health management, and entertainment.

The journey through the evolution of wearable tech has illuminated the significant strides made in design and aesthetics. Wearables are no longer limited to clunky, utilitarian devices but have become fashion-forward accessories that users proudly incorporate into their outfits. The collaboration between fashion designers and technologists has been instrumental in creating wearables that appeal to diverse tastes, empowering users to express their individuality while enjoying the benefits of technology.

The successful case studies of fashionable wearables showcased how user-centric design and aesthetically appealing features have driven the commercial success of wearable tech. By understanding the desires and preferences of consumers, wearables have seamlessly integrated into our lives, blending into our style choices without compromising on functionality.

Moreover, the functionality aspect of wearables has been a driving force behind their widespread adoption. From health and fitness wearables that empower users to take charge of their well-being to smart garments that offer interactive experiences, wearables have enriched our lives in numerous ways.

The integration of AI and data has been transformative, providing personalized insights, coaching, and recommendations that cater to individual needs and preferences. However, this progress has also raised ethical considerations concerning data privacy, transparency, and accountability. As we look ahead, the responsible development and use of wearable tech will be crucial to maintaining user trust and ensuring that wearable technology continues to be a force for positive change.

The future of wearable technology holds boundless potential. We envision wearables that seamlessly blend with our clothing, becoming invisible yet powerful tools that augment our daily experiences. Health monitoring will reach new heights with wearables capable of detecting health issues proactively, paving the way for preventive care and personalized treatment plans.

The fusion of fashion and functionality will continue to drive innovation in the wearables industry, fostering creativity, and improving user experiences. Smart fashion and interactive clothing will redefine how we express ourselves, offering a canvas for self-expression that seamlessly incorporates technology into our identity.

As wearable tech evolves, it will become an even more integral part of our lives, shaping how we interact with technology, each other, and the world around us. It will empower us to lead healthier lives, enhance our entertainment experiences, and connect with the digital realm in ways that are both meaningful and seamless.

In conclusion, the fusion of fashion and functionality in wearable technology has given rise to a new era of digital innovation. By marrying style with substance, wearables have transcended mere gadgets to become extensions of our identity and aspirations. As we embrace the challenges and possibilities of wearable tech's future, we must prioritize ethical considerations and responsible design to ensure that wearable technology remains a beacon of progress, enriching our lives and shaping a more connected and empowered future for all.

C. Inspiring Readers to Embrace the Potential of Wearable Tech:

As we conclude our journey through the world of wearable technology, we hope to leave you, our readers, inspired and excited about the immense potential that wearables hold. The fusion of fashion and functionality in these innovative devices opens up a world of possibilities, empowering individuals to lead healthier, more connected, and technologically enriched lives.

Wearable tech is no longer a futuristic concept. It is here, now, and it is transforming the way we interact with technology and the world around us. Whether it's a stylish smartwatch that keeps you connected and organized or a fitness tracker that motivates you to reach your health goals, wearables have become indispensable companions in our modern lives.

Imagine a future where wearable health devices continuously monitor your vital signs, providing early warnings of potential health issues, and enabling preventive care. Envision garments that respond to your body's needs, regulating temperature or adjusting fit for optimal comfort and performance. Picture a world where wearable AR contact lenses enhance your vision with information and digital overlays, making navigation and communication effortless.

The potential of wearable tech to enhance mental health is equally promising. Wearables could detect stress levels and provide tailored relaxation techniques or mindfulness exercises to promote emotional well-being. These devices could become personal coaches, empowering you to achieve a balanced lifestyle and manage stress effectively.

Wearable technology has the power to revolutionize entertainment and gaming, providing immersive experiences that blur the lines between the virtual and physical worlds. Imagine being part of interactive stories where your choices shape the narrative, or gaming experiences where you physically engage in virtual battles and quests.

The convergence of fashion and functionality in wearables is reshaping the relationship between technology and personal style. Wearables are no longer merely tools; they are extensions of ourselves, reflecting our tastes and aspirations. Embrace wearables as an opportunity to express your individuality, integrating them seamlessly into your daily fashion choices.

As you embrace the potential of wearable tech, remember the importance of responsible use and ethical considerations. Advocate for transparent data practices, user privacy, and inclusivity in wearable design. Support initiatives that promote accessibility and empower users to control their data and wearable experiences.

In this ever-evolving landscape of wearable technology, your feedback and ideas matter. Engage with wearable tech communities, share your experiences, and provide insights to shape the future of wearable devices. Advocate for wearables that align with your values and needs, encouraging manufacturers to create products that resonate with diverse users.

Let wearable tech be a catalyst for positive change in your life. Embrace it as a tool that enhances your well-being, productivity, and entertainment experiences. Be open to exploring new wearables and technologies, as they have the potential to unlock new dimensions of convenience, connectivity, and self-discovery.

In conclusion, wearable technology is not just a passing trend; it is a transformative force that will continue to shape the way we live, work, and play. Embrace the fusion of fashion and functionality, and let wearable tech become an empowering and enriching part of your life's journey. As you embrace this ever-evolving tech frontier, dare to dream of a future where wearable technology unlocks possibilities beyond imagination, making your life not only smarter but also more inspired and fulfilling.